PUBLISHED BY

Kirkbymoorside History Group 2014

COPYRIGHT © KIRKBYMOORSIDE HISTORY GROUP
2014

NO PART OF THIS PUBLICATION MAY BE
REPRODUCED OR TRANSMITTED IN ANY FORM
WITHOUT PRIOR WRITTEN PERMISSION OF THE
COPYRIGHT OWNER.

ISBN 978-0-9564745-9-9

PRINTED BY

HPE PRINT
THORNTON ROAD
INDUSTRIAL ESTATE
PICKERING
NORTH YORKSHIRE
YO18 7JB

TEL: 01751 473578

Other titles available from the Kirkbymoorside History Group

Adela Shaw and The Yorkshire Children's Orthopaedic Hospital

Smile... Snapshots from the wards

Fresh Air on the Verandah

All Saints Through The Ages

"Kirkbymoorside Proudly Presents..."

Boot Polish and Blanco

The Millers of Kirkbymoorside

Digging For Yennits

The title of our latest minglement book came from a childhood name for hawthorn leaves, folded over and eaten - known as 'bread and cheese'.

It is a collection of childhood tales, recorded by residents who came from the villages closely linked to the town such as Rudland and Harome as well as Kirkbymoorside itself. We hope you enjoy the stories and perhaps some of you will recognise your own childhood days; not everything has changed...

Harry Ward

Harry Ward was born in May 1923, one of three siblings from Harome. His father John Ward (1894 -1976) worked on Ryehope Farm, at Harome and went on to purchase it for £200 in 1926, (following a legacy of £100 left to him by William Bulmer). His father was also involved in various groups and acted as secretary, proud of his wonderful handwriting. He was given a mantelpiece clock with an inscribed plaque on commemorating 25 years service to the British Legion. The village could always field two cricket teams and they would all be local lads. John would act as umpire for the local cricket teams and enjoyed sharing in the teams' victories but was not one for actually playing.

Not wanting to follow his father's passion of scholarly pursuits, Harry was keen to leave the village school as soon as he reached the age of 14. The local school was popular and had around 30 pupils, with two school gardens; one was next door and the other a little further away near the Star Inn, now the site of a bungalow.

One of his first jobs, he recalls, was pulling plums for Marsar Ellerker who lived at the bottom of West End in Kirkby-moorside and who had large fruit orchards at the rear as well as owning land near Malton Road. A group of three or four boys would go along to pull fruit from the trees supervised by Jack Anderson and Reg Davison. Mr Ellerker was a cantankerous gentleman and the boys were wary of him. When WWII broke out Reg Davison was called up. He returned injured having lost a leg. Undeterred, Reg moved back to Nawton and set up a shoe repair shop in Station Road.

Harry's first job was with Mr Rickatson at Summerfields Farm, where he looked after the poultry and pigs, a job he loved, apart from ringing the pigs' noses. He was paid 10

Shillings a week. From this he had to pay his mother for board and food.

Harry riding the middle horse at Summerfields Farm.

In March 1939, Harry bought a new bike. It had three gears and was very modern, costing him £6-19-6d.

At the age of 15 he came home to learn his father had hired him to Walter Marwood for the year, not a job he had wanted, but he was not in a position to argue.

This was from the November hirings in 1939. His wage was eight shillings per week, but he lived in. At the end of his first year, he was paid the sum of £21- he remembered being paid with the Big White £5 notes. When he got home (as pleased as punch) his father said he would get his book out. This was the book where Harry's father had kept a tally of the costs he had incurred over the year. He owed for clothing, shoes and the bike. Poor Harry had to hand over everything and was still in debt. In his second year at the Marwoods he was paid 10/6 a week each month.

Harry recalls hearing the declaration of war on the radio; the family didn't have one so he went over to his grandmother's house and joined the dozen or so residents who had all gathered to hear the announcement in her front room.

Keen to do his bit, he and a few other lads set off one morning to join up in Helmsley. The group were stopped by his father who told them in no uncertain terms to 'wait until they want you' – he had tears in his eyes as he told the lads, they had no idea what they were about to walk into.

Harry's dad, John, had served in the Green Howards during WWI and had seen his own cousin Fred, killed beside him in Belgium, aged 22. Fred is buried in Maple Copse Cemetery, Leper, West-Vlaanderen, Belgium.

Traumatised by the action he had seen, his discharge papers listed stress as one of the injuries received, and probably accounted for his father's demeanour, who was quick to anger and easily worked up about things.

So instead the lads joined the Home Guard. Harome would join forces with Nunnington, and the troop would go off on manoeuvres and training camps. He remembers the adventures they got up to. To begin with the group didn't have rifles, but paraded with sticks. In true Dad's Army fashion they would have to bike with these 'weapons' over their shoulders to the camps. They would sleep under canvas on palliasses (mattresses filled with straw) and on occasion dried thistles, which would make themselves felt through the material. On one occasion, when the guards were up on manoeuvres at Skellamoor above Pickering, the Harome lads discovered a goat tethered beside the road and pinched it. The Nunnington boys who were in a nearby tent, woke to find this goat inside, having been thrust through the tent flap. Needless to say those involved got into severe trouble for that prank. In charge of the division was Capt. Holt (later to be promoted to Colonel) whilst leading Harome Home Guards was Mr Black, a gamekeeper from Harome, who was Lieutenant. Tom Field and Mr Ward Snr were the sergeants with Billy Shields and Ernest Dodds the corporals. There were about 26 men in total.

Harry was in charge of a Browning machine gun along with Walter Lawson and Bernard Rickatson, and remembers being up at Beck Dale and having to use water to cool it down, otherwise the bullets boiled if they went through too fast. Another close shave came one day when the Home Guards were on their way down Cauklees Bank when someone managed to drop a live hand grenade. The pin came out and Sgt Major Bayes had to grab it quick and throw it into the field before it exploded.

Duncombe Park was the venue for a large manoeuvre and Harry and Bernard were on guard duty. They challenged a group of officers, who approached them and not getting the right password they held them there and refused to let them enter. It was some time before the group, who turned out to be visiting high ranking officers, were ushered through with some embarrassment - no-one could blame Harry and Bernard, as no password meant no entry.

Walter Marwood had a mixed farm, like most in the area, so Harry would get up and do the milking from 7 am before going into the farmhouse for breakfast. Mrs Marwood was

Harome Home Guard 1944 Harry Ward - middle row fourth from left

11

Proud parents Harry and Lydia

kind to the youngster, but Harry recalls Walter would come in and stare at the farm clock as if to say, *Hurry it Up*, and Harry would be back out working the horses finishing about six o'clock at night.

The farm had cattle and two shire horses. He remembers braiding their manes and tails with ribbons and dressing them with harness and brasses. As there was no other entertainment and a chance of a break from work, the farm lads would be expected to attend church. In those days, at least three pews in the small church would be filled with farm hands alone. Harry worked for two years for Mr Marwood, but when it came time for his third year he was let go, as the increase in wage would be too high. He worked there   November 1940 – 1942.

He then went to work for Mr Fairburn, at Long Woods Farm in Nawton. Mr Fairburn was a gentleman. He had hunting horses, cows and pigs. These horses were also used for work.   Harry delivered the milk to the army. On one occasion he arrived and the 'Unit' had been changed. He didn't know the new password and was obliged to spent time in the guards hut, while everything was sorted out.

He cycled from Harome to Nawton twice on Saturdays and Sundays for milking. He was living at home and also did some gardening while working at Mr Fairburn's farm.

He was once asked to stay at the farm, as a mare was in foal. He spent two weeks waiting for the arrival. Mr Fairburn told him to go home and get some rest. Typical - next morning, when Harry arrived, there was the foal.

There was a tractor at Fairburn's farm during the time Harry was there.

Harry left Fairburn's employment when the lime, stored in the barn, started leaking from the paper bags it was stored in. This caused blistering and sores to break out on the farm hands and horses alike. It became unbearable.

Harry with a dressed horse, WWII Gala, Harome

Harry then went to work for Mr Albert Houlson at Laurel's Farm in Harome. Mr Houlson was a good stockman and a good boss. He worked there for nine years. From November 1942 – Nov 1951. He was employed as horseman and worked on the land. The first tractor in the village arrived in 1942, at Laurel's Farm. Despite having worked as a horseman, the lure of new technology was great and when a tractor was bought everyone was keen to try it out. Too young for a full driving licence, Harry was given a permit to drive from 'one farm to another'. This was the wording on the document.

Along with the war came the evacuees from Hull and Middlesbrough, many came to Harome but the Ward family didn't have the room to take any in. The longest to stay was a Barry Ward (no relation) from Stockton; he had a lame leg and eventually returned home after the war and would open a shop. He was exceptionally good at batting when playing cricket, but unable to run fast.

As well as evacuees, a ready supply of labour was found in the form of prisoners of war from nearby Eden Camp. As they were unable to speak English, Harry found himself responsible for instructing these men through hand signals, often by pointing to the tractor. Not many caused trouble; most were resigned or even relieved by their new occupation. Over the years the farm took on Germans, Italians and even Polish POWs. They would be dropped off in a morning with a large dry 'doorstep' sandwich for lunch and gathered up on a night-time. More often than not the farmers took pity and supplemented their meagre rations.

One German POW made an impression – he was called Johnny Hahn and came to work with Harry from Eden Camp. One day he pointed to a molehill and mimed painting. Eventually it was established that Johnny was asking for velvet (like the skin of a mole). Harry got a piece of black velvet from his grandmother, taken from a dress belonging to her mother, and brought it in. In a very short space of time, Johnny returned the velvet to Harry having used it as a canvas for a painting of a scene from the Black Forest, showing a castle standing above a lake. Johnny also made his son, Keith, a hand held wooden toy – one with chickens pecking the ground as a ball swings underneath.

When the war finished they exchanged addresses but they never heard from him. Around the same time as Eden Camp closed down and POWs were shipped out, a train crashed outside Doncaster carrying POWs down to London to be repatriated home and so Johnny's story remains unknown.

Harome was sheltered from the worst of the war in many ways. There were two shops in the village and rations were supplemented by the farms round about. Pigs were raised in back yards and the area was full of small family run mixed farms. Not that farmers' sons were any better off than the workers, they would often have to beg and borrow to make ends meet as did everyone else – 'never a penny in their pockets' – that summed up their position.

Harome Coronation Fancy Dress Parade May 12/37

Harry remembers the gunning of Kirby main street by a lone bomber on August Bank Holiday in 1943 and the bullet marks which were left in the brickwork near Tinley Garth. There had been an event in Kirkby that day.

The nearest the war came to Harome was during one night when incendiary bombs were dropped. Having already hit Welburn Hall which was being used as a hospital, the bombs fell in Harome village. Harry returned from seeing Lydia up at Harome Heads to see the hedge outside his house on fire and Ernest Dodds frantically trying to put out the fire in his thatched roof - luckily Ernest was the fire warden. The incendiaries burned with a distinct glow that Harry can still recall in the back garden – a real bright white ball of flame.

Wombleton aerodrome was close by and attracted many workers who built the site and Canadian airmen were based there. Harry was a keen billiard player and would visit the

John Ward as
standard bearer

Reading Rooms in Kirkby to play. One worker from Wombleton aerodrome, despite having one arm, was a keen billiard player and would use his cap folded up as the rest for his cue, quickly swiping the cap back before the ball hit it. Another billiard player that Harry met was an RAF Officer whose father owned billiard halls in London. He wouldn't even start playing until the score had built up and once he got onto the table, no-one else got a shot in. He was marvellous to watch.

It was during WWII that Harry met Lydia. With the onset of war, women were expected to work. She had gone for a job interview with the Shepherd family at Brandsby and on the way home had missed her lift and she along with her sister Kathleen, had to walk from Helmsley to Kirkbymoorside before making it back home to Cropton.

When the sisters finally got home, her father said that Mr Strickland had rung to see if she would go and work on his farm at Harome Heads as a land girl. That was how she came to Harome and to meet Harry. It was after one church service that Harry met his future wife, Lydia Fletcher.

Harry and Lydia went to ENSA (Entertainments National Service Association) concerts held at the aerodrome, where locals and soldiers would go to see variety shows. These ENSA concerts were created especially to entertain the troops during WWII and many successful, well known actors and comedians began their careers at this time.

Lydia lived at Beck House in Cropton, having been born in Spaunton The family lived for a time in Rosedale, which was where Lydia went to school. The family moved to Beck House, when her father went to work as a cowman. After three years of chilblains working in the fields as a land girl,

Lydia finally got to change career to that of a housewife and mother. On 6th January 1945 Lydia and Harry married in Lastingham Church. They set up home in Harome living in rooms on the Main Street, belonging to Bertie Flintoff. They then moved into the 'Airey' (prefab) houses in Knavesmire Close. Imagine Lydia's surprise and horror when the curtains she put up in their first home together were mirrored by the Shields who lived in the house directly opposite!

In 1951 Harry went to the Feversham Estate and worked in many areas, from Beadlam Grange to Pennyholme. He would thin copses of trees, deliver wooden huts and do general farm work. He worked where he was told and did what he was asked, there was no question of having a job description!

He drove the tractor, which was filled at Bulmers Petrol station, next to the Feathers Hotel in Helmsley. It would hold between four and five gallons of petrol and had to be signed for. An account was then sent to the Feversham Estate at the end of the month.

Steam powered council wagon, driven by Artie Smith

Harry would cycle from Harome to Helmsley for a 7 am start. Workers gathered behind the Feversham Arms in Hutchinson's Agricultural Engineers yard. The daily work was from 7 am – 5 pm. Their 'allowance' break was 10 minutes in the morning and a ½ hour break for lunch. The workers brought a 'pack out' from home. Harry worked closely with a man from Helmsley called Billy Scobie.

In 1956 the Feversham Estate decided to let Rye House. Still working for the Feversham Estate, Harry, being a foreman, was offered another house - Beadlam Grange.

In 1962, Lord Feversham decided to reduce the Estate. The family spent a couple of weeks in a cottage in Rievaulx, whilst looking for other employment. Colonel Edgerton recommended Harry to Sir William Brookesbank, who had land near Westow. When Harry and Lydia went to see the cottage they had been offered with the job, Lydia was slightly concerned about the distance the children would have to go to school along winding and narrow roads. The cottage was inside the cut off boundary for bus transfers to and from school. It would have been a long way for the children – 6, 9 and 12 to walk every morning and evening. They did not take up this position. They then went to see Mr Sherbrooke, out Stamford Bridge way. The cottage they were offered was too small, so they were offered a farm-house. This was in very damp and in bad condition.

Harry then applied to the Ravenswick Estate and was offered the job of farm foreman. With the job came some accommodation at Sinnington Manor, which was owned by Colonel Holt and where they would live for the next 26 years. A big rambling house, kept spotless by Lydia. The family were very happy and settled here. One incident whilst the family lived there, made the national newspapers. Although the farm belonged to Colonel Holt, access to it was across Wardle Darley's land and a fine had to be paid to him to even set foot on it.

One year the fine was increased and Colonel Holt refused to pay. The first Harry and Lydia knew was when the barbed wire was put up across the farm gates and the lane to the main road was closed off. With three children to collect from school, a Land rover was dispatched from Holts Farm to collect them and the family had to use a back road, Shaw Lane, to get in and out of the property. Harry remembers the Northern Echo journalist Diana Walters who took up the story. Later, even the Daily Telegraph told the tale of the family who were wired into their own home. Eventually the dispute was settled and the wire came down.

Harry retired in 1988 and, with Lydia, moved to Kirkbymoorside. They lived in Bridge Bungalow on Ings Lane until they moved to Manor Close in April 1997.

Patricia Kew
celebrating her
100th birthday
in 2013

Interview with **Patricia May Kew (née Pilmoor) - 2013**

"I was born on 17th March 1913 at 12 Castlegate in Kirkbymoorside, the youngest of a family of eight; James, Elizabeth, Margaret, Kate, Sarah, Samuel, Veronica and then me. My mother was called Hannah Magee and her father ran a ship's chandler's shop in Crown Square, now home to Busy Liz's flowers. The building later was used as a garage and then left derelict. Later it was renovated and they found a date stone set into it which read 1724, but the porcelain sign which was intact, was taken down.

My father – Samuel Pilmoor - ran a barber's shop down in the Market place in premises that joined onto the Black Swan porch; it was only narrow and room was at a premium there. Later the shop was absorbed by Maw's Stores and then became part of Thomas the Baker's. Dad sadly died when I was only two and my mum had to bring us up alone.

Dad's barber's shop

The house in Castlegate was a small two up two down property typical of the cottages which in days gone by had housed weavers. I do remember water coming to the properties, but originally we had to fetch water from the pump which was located at the bottom of Castlegate on the left-hand side set back from the road. When water did arrive, it wasn't into the house but into the back yard and was still shared by several households. I remember Mum filling the wooden washing tub up the night before wash day so that the wood could swell and become waterproof. One of my earliest memories of Castlegate was seeing the First World War soldiers who were camped up at the Park Field (right at the top as if you were going to Rumsgill) in large canvas tents, marching down to the main square and I can clearly recall seeing the puttees on their legs and all the children running alongside them. My brother Jim (below) served during the Great War and fought at the Somme. Remarkable he met someone from Kirby both of them covered in mud. Thankfully Jim returned home safely.

Mr & Mrs Sleightholme lived next door to us with Gerry and Helen (they later moved into Reservoir Cottage) and above that was Brewster's Farm; I can still see the cattle and sheep being driven down from the farm to the auction mart at the bottom. We used to get our milk from Brewster's. Kirk Warren would come round with a horse and cart and a milk churn and he would scoop it into Mum's milk jug. The road was only made of dirt in those days. The only solid areas were the large flagstones along the road side, forming the pavement. I remember we would play on those flags for hours outside Low Hall. Cath Boddy, Mary Proud, Jane Sturdy and I would all play Hop Scotch and Six Square Hop, and of course there was always knocking on doors in Dale

End. Jane's family ran the Workhouse up at the top of Dale End – we never really went up there, it was too scary a place for children. A Miss Revely lived at Low Hall and she gave music and piano lessons; Cath Boddy used to go there to learn music. Fletcher's lived opposite Low Hall.

We would stand for ages and watch the blacksmith, Mr Hodgson, at work in his forge at the bottom of Castlegate. He would shoe horses and it was always a fascinating and busy place for us kids. Another small thing – there were lots of owls nesting in the trees between High Hall and Low Hall. From my bedroom I would mimic them and they would answer back!

There wasn't much traffic in those days and we had the best street to sledge down. We used to sled from the top to bottom of the street and would have landed up in the station if we'd let it go. Mum would never let me warm my hands in front of the open fire after I had been outside playing in the snow. She said it would give me chilblains. But I was allowed to warm them in a bowl of hot water.

Life wasn't easy for Mum, but most of my older siblings had left school and gone onto work by the time I was growing up. We were never hungry as children, there were always good home-cooked meals, and as a Sunday treat Mum would say to us "If you behave yourselves, I'll make you some toffee!"

Manor Vale was another haven for us children to play in. We would play for hours on the Swinging Tree – which was an old tree that had fallen forward we would sit on the trunk and swing on the branches, a little way down from the Castle Wall. We would go past the bowling green on the right hand side and see Mr Lealman at the rope walk on the left. We used to play in and around the huge long sheds where they wound the ropes. And of course there was always egg collecting and bird nesting; the Manor Vale was very different then.

When we wanted to collect wood, we would go up Rumsgill to get a bodin of sticks, which we carried home on our heads. Rumsgill was a great place for all kinds of things. The First Bank was where we gathered wild strawberries; we would always go to Rumsgill to collect brambles and gale to make gale beer. Not many people seem to remember it; it tasted lovely, but it was such a volatile mixture. So many times we heard the bang as the glass bottles upstairs exploded when the yeast had fermented too much.

I went to the Kirby School at the age of five.

I remember some of my schoolmates; Cath Boddy, Kath Strickland, Edith King and the Allanby boys. One of them broke his leg; we were coming out of school and he jumped up onto the back of a horse and cart in Tinley Garth and fell off. On our way down to school we would call in at Hutchinson's shop for a ½ d or 1 d worth of sweets, or perhaps an orange. Our headmaster was Mr Donkin and there was Miss Nash and about four other teachers. They taught us according to age groups and we studied the usual subjects - Maths, English, Geography, History and Cookery. The police station was next door and the Congregational Church was a bit further down Tinley Garth.

I enjoyed school, and on a Thursday a teacher would come along to teach us cookery. One time we made pancakes and Cathy and I were allowed one and sneakily put some sugar on it to eat. Trouble was we had put salt on it by mistake!

The town itself was pretty much unchanged from today apart from the number of shops. We had a butcher's in Dale End, Mr Taylor's, where they used to slaughter the animals down the yard and Waind's in the Market Place. I remember going into Waind's as a little girl with my mum to get meat – they had all sons I recall. I went in recently and was served by the grandson of the Reg Waind, who served my mum. I also remember Mr Walker in his tiny cobbler's workshop in Crown Square; the floor was sandstone and sloped down. He would be surrounded by boots and shoes, working away in the corner on a small stool. It was always filled with the smell of leather and glue.

We used to go to the new cinema which was started by Mr Ben Blackburn and was a large vehicle-type machine which joined onto the back of the hall. Ivy his daughter was a lovely person and played the music to go with the films. I can still see Mr Proud, Mary's dad, who was our neighbour in Castlegate and he used to clean the windows at the King's Head Hotel. Below that there was the water pump on the hill near the old vicarage opposite the Memorial Hall.

The other important event in the week was going to church. We went to St Chad's and I was baptised there, with Mrs Mary Conning acting as my godmother. There were very few families at that time that went to the Catholic Church – Miss Clark, the Reeds from West End, Watsons, Stockdales and Connings were the families I recall attending regularly with us, the Pilmoor family; a Miss Mozzotti, who was already a very old lady from Kirby Mills when I was a girl, taught us the catechisms; we always had to have our tidy clothes on for Mass. The priest had to come from Ampleforth and only on a Sunday. We had a Father Joseph Smith, who would come through from Ampleforth on his motorbike, wearing his cap back to front and flying goggles. He would sometimes bring a Father Basil Hulme as his pillion passenger, later to be Cardinal Hulme. Whenever I am in Kirby I still go to Wednesday mass.

St Chad's interior

All the local children used to go on a Sunday School trip to Scarborough, once a year, paid for by the churches. But as the Catholic community and church were so small, they couldn't afford to pay and so the parents had to pay themselves. I told my mum I knew I wouldn't be able to go. She was determined that I could and took an extra job, scrubbing the floors of Blakey's shop (opposite the George & Dragon) to pay for my trip.

I can remember the town bier being used. It would collect the coffin from the family's home and then wheeled down the street to the churchyard; its wheels were muffled with ropes and all the houses would draw their curtains as it passed by as a mark of respect.

Times were so different then, we never had to worry about locking our doors. Everyone was the same and we all helped one another. The postman who came round with any mail would carry, as I remember, a small carbine light as there were no street lights then. If no-one was home, he would simply open the front door and leave the letters on the table. No-one thought anything of it. We always had a cat in the house; there were always plenty of litters being born in Castlegate, on shed roofs and back gardens. The cat was always allowed to stay in during the day, but come night-time, I remember Mum would gently nudge him up the three steps into the back yard with her foot and the cat would be out for the night.

Hiring time meant the fair would come to Kirbymoorside, usually around Martinmas. The market place was full of stalls, carousel, roundabouts and swing-boats. I particularly enjoyed a ride called the cake walk, which was a kind of moving platform. Once you got the hang of it, it was great, but until you did, it threw you all over the place. I only remember the men waiting for work, but as children we didn't really take any notice.

Mrs Adela Shaw's mother was the local Girl Guide captain in Kirby and we would go to the Church House for meetings. Years later my daughter became friends with Tony Simpson, son of Ron (right) who worked as secretary at the hospital. We would help Ron hand out presents to the children in hospital at Christmas if we were in town.

As a teenager, I would go to the dances in town. The New Year's Eve Dance was the highlight for me, in the Memorial

Hall. But we would also go to the 6 d hops at the Church House and there was also a large room above Waind's shop, at the back, which they hired out for dances as well.

When I left school at the age of 12, there was not much choice of things to do; most went into farming or domestic service. In 1930 I went to join my sister who was married and living in York, to go to work at Terry's Confectionary. In the end I went to work at Bough's Fashions. I would come home to visit on the train. Kirbymoorside Station was a lovely little place, but so cold. Maud Rutter and I would travel home together on a Friday and during the war I remember the vast numbers of soldiers filling the platform and carriages heading back from leave on a Monday back into York.

I have always thought of Kirkbymoorside as my home. When my husband Harry was alive we would come over quite often. I still visit with my daughter now and we always buy our meat from Wainds still. On one occasion, I met up with the Brown twins, whose father had the garage at the bottom of the town. They said "Harry Rickaby is over there, go talk to him." Harry was a student teacher in Kirkby Primary School when I was there and taught our class before he left. I didn't believe he would remember me, but as soon as I saw him, he said "By God, you're wearing well!" He recognised me immediately and said "You tell your friends there are not many 92 year old students who can say that they have been talking to their 96 year old teacher." He was a lovely man.

It was thanks to him I have a beautiful painting of Castlegate. Harry and I came through and saw the local Art Club Exhibition in Church House and on display was a watercolour showing Castlegate. It wasn't for sale and Harry said he would have a word with the artist, Helen Pierson, to see if she would sell it to us. Thankfully she did and it still hangs in my bedroom now. In the picture there is a figure walking up the road, back to us which I know is Reg Waind. For some reason everyone called him Katie – he was a bit of a lone figure.

My sister, Margaret Pilmoor, used to work at the school canteen with Mrs Jones, Mrs Hornby, Mrs Gill and Mrs Ward in the old asbestos building, which served all the village schools, cooked and delivered from Kirkby. It was recently dismantled and replaced with the new play group building outside the town primary school.

Sam Pilmoor (Pat's father) shaving Joe Proud with a saw!

One other small thing I've never forgotten is learning an inscription from an old gravestone on the corner of the All Saints churchyard. I can still recite it today:

> 'Remember man, as you pass by
> As you are now so once was I
> As I am now, so you shall be
> So be prepared to follow me.'

Strange the things you remember."

Families Listed in 1911 Census for Rudland

Surname	Address
Atkinson	Cherry Tree Farm, Sleightholme Dale
Champion	Hope Inn
Dandy	School Row
Denney	Sleights House
Fawbert	School Row
Fletcher James	Sykes House
Fletcher Thomas	White Sykes
Green	Sykes Cottage, Fadmoor
Kay	Sykes House, Fadmoor
Powell	Sleightholme Dale
Richardson	Grey's Farm, Fadmoor
Teasdale Isaac	Stonely Woods
Teasdale James	Poverty Cottage
Walkington	Allotments House
Wardell	The Spa, Sleightholme Dale
Waudby	Penny Holme
Wildsmith	Aumbry House,
Willoughby	Common Cottage
Wilson	Common Cottage

Teasdale Family Tree

Isaac Henry **Teasdale**   (1870 - 1952)
married Elizabeth **Walkington** (1871 - 1958)

Herbert   (1891 - 1983)

Robert Jeremiah   (1894 - 1978)

Lily   (1895 - 1987)

Ellen Jane Elizabeth   (1897 - 1989)

Harry Lund   (1899 - 1984)

Frederick   (1900 - 1983)

William Henry   (1902 - 1951)

Violet   (1904 - 1999)

Thomas Isaac   (1907 - 1989)

Strickland   (1909 - 1985)

Rose May (1913 - 2014) —- Thomas Percival **Magson**
                                           (1909 -1974)

Jackson   (1916 - 1995)

Shirley —— Robert **Avison**

Kathleen —— Peter **Robinson**

Rosie, with her daughter Kathleen, her grand-daughter
Bridget and great grand-daughter Grace, at Kirkbymoorside's
Diamond Jubilee event in 2012.

Rosie's Story

Rosie's dad, Isaac Henry Teasdale, came from a family who had lived in the Rudland area since the 1830s when Joseph Teasdale (her great grandfather) came to work at a coal mine along with his brother George. The family settled at Penny Holme and later generations turned to farming as these shallow mines became exhausted.

In 1891 Isaac married Elizabeth Walkington and they settled into Stonely Woods, where they would raise a large family and survive on the land. Rosie was born in November 1913, second youngest of eight boys and four girls.

She was told that when news came to the village of her birth, George Simpson from the Gillamoor Post Office, asked if he could be allowed to name her. George had never married and her parents also agreed to him acting as her godfather, which was a first for any of the Teasdale children. So she became Rose May and received a small bible as well as her name at the christening in the Gillamoor church.

Rudland, high up above Fadmoor, was an isolated community and the once healthy population boosted by the mining activities had dwindled and those now living here were dependant on the land for their livelihood. The field names show how hard the locals had found working the land in the past - Poverty, Beggeration and Hunger Hill. The moor coal found around Harland Head and Rudland was used in the lime kilns at Mill Bank and Sleightholme Dale. The dales and moors offered a living, but it was not an easy option.

With no mains water supply or electricity for heating or cooking, the family all had to work together to ensure they gathered what they needed. The family farm was around 50 acres and they grew potatoes, grain and hay for cattle, livestock including pigs, sheep, cows as well as the usual hens, ducks, geese and horses.

For Rosie, school was a happy time in her life, although not necessarily the schoolwork it involved. She never liked history or geography. The school was only small, with 15 pupils in her day and was only a field away from the family farm. All the children were in one room with the bigger children sitting at the back and the little ones at the front. Some pupils, such as Tom Fletcher, would have to walk a mile and few even came from as far away as Skiplam, which is five miles away. In winter the school would be shut if the snow was heavy, which suited the children just fine!

Rudland School, 1927.

The uniform for the girls was a white starched pinny over their everyday clothes and all the children studied in the one classroom, which was heated by an open fire. Those who lived far away, brought a pack-up for dinner, but Rosie could run home and back in the hour they had.

The school teacher was 'Old' Mrs Hammond, who also lived locally. Rosie remembered she kept goats and smelt of them; she was a real strict teacher and there was no messing about in her school. She would often threaten to 'clatter 'em' if they misbehaved; any trouble in school was soon heard about by the rest of the village. That meant no hiding it from your parents, which also meant another telling off at home. Mrs John Denney was another teacher, but she was far more easy-going and in Tom's day the school gained a reputation of being rather unruly.

Stonely Woods, Rudland

Tom remembered being 'on the carpet' over an escapade with Rosie's dad's sheepdog. The dog came up each dinnertime in hope of a few tit-bits and the lads decided to tie a treacle tin to his tail. The dog set off and headed home to Stonely Woods, dragging the tin and making a real racket. Unfortunately Mr Teasdale was not only a parent, but a school governor, so, for the lads, punishment was inevitable.

At play-time the children would disappear in all directions to play games such as fox-off and would roam the fields and woods, up onto Boon Hill top, which was ½ mile away. Getting them back for the afternoon session was not always easy; especially if they were out of hearing distance of the school whistle. To try and solve this one, the teacher would put out a cloth on the fence when it was time to come back, but the lads soon cottoned onto the fact she put it out five minutes early to try and get them back on time!

The caretaker was Ada, Mrs Jim Fletcher from Sykes House, and she had to walk through the wood to get to work.

For anyone caught talking in class, the cane and ruler would be brought into action. Rosie was never caned, but the boys had a trick to try and avoid it. The teacher would hold their wrist, so instead of pulling their hand away, the boy would push it towards the teacher and often she would bring the ruler down on her own hand! Lines at playtime was another common punishment, along with a slap round 'your lug-'ole' when you weren't listening!

The boys also were regulars at creating and flicking blotting paper balls up onto the ceiling, where they would stick courtesy of the spit used to create them. When the school mistress saw them up there, her response was 'I didn't know the school top had measles!' The treatment was for the lads to get the telescopic brush and sweep them off the ceiling and then from the floor, all during play-time of course.

On a Saturday morning, Rosie's Dad would heat up the copper in the old wash-house he used as a bit of blacksmith's shop and fill it with taties for the pigs. These would then be tipped into the old stone trough and, using a posser, mashed them up with barley and oatmeal to fatten up the pigs. However Rosie and her friends could tell by the reek from the chimney what he was doing and would sneak over the fields and pinch a few to eat hot. The boys would grab one or two and play tricks on the girls, touching their legs with the hot potato to make them scream.

For sports day occasionally they would bring the children down into Kirby to join up with the other village schools, as there would not be much competition with only a dozen or so pupils.

Rosie had to leave school early, as after the summer break in her final year, the school was closed for six months following a really bad outbreak of measles. So she never got back, although by that stage she was ready to be away.

On the farm, life was hard work. Water supplies came from a stream-fed stone trough, which then filled a second and was the only source of water for both the people and stock on the farm. They had to carry it in buckets to get it into the house. In the hotter weather, the stream would slow to a trickle and her dad would have to dig down to try and increase the supply. 'Dad often said to go careful with that water' as there was nowhere else to go for it. Outside, next to the stone trough, there was a slabstone which came out of the wall and on it was set a bowl ready to fill with water when needed. In wintertime the problem was the water freezing in the troughs and her dad would have to break the ice every morning and keep an eye on it through the day.

Typical farmhouse fire and oven

Work began with dawn and the feeding of the family's stock; the cows would be milked and it was Rosie's job to pour it into a separator and turn the handle. This would split it into milk at one side and cream the other. The milk would go to feed the calves and the family, whilst the cream was used to make butter and cheese. Monday was butter churning day, after Mam had done the washing.

They didn't make a lot of cheese, but what they made a was good; it was a white cheese, a bit like Wensleydale.

Washing day was always Monday and meant lots of water needed to fill a very large pan, which held two full buckets itself, as well as the side boiler. The sheets had to be boiled in the pan and Mam also had to ladle hot water out of the boiler with a tin to wash the family's clothes. They didn't wash as often as today, because water was so precious and it was such hard work. Another daily chore was baking. Her mam would bake seven loaves of bread on a Friday in the great old fire oven. She also made a host of other pies, fruit cakes and scones.

Rosie remembered that they always had butter and treacle on the sad cakes and scones.

Her mam's recipe for the sad cakes was quite simple: flour, baking powder, lard and a bit of cold water to mix it to a dough. This was flattened out to the size of a dinner plate and baked. Once done, she would split and cover with butter and treacle. After the baking session, she would put a lump of home-cured salt bacon in the hot oven, which created a lovely smell that drifted over the yard. That was good in itself, but the bacon tasted great.

The flour for all this baking was bought in 10 stone sacks at a time and kept in a bin near the fire to keep it dry. The flour came from one of the millers in Kirbymoorside and was brought up by horse and cart.

One time of year which caused her mother even more work was harvest and haytime, when she had to provide lowances for the men in the fields every day. They needed a regular supply of scones, apple pies, fruit cake, jam and fruit puffs along with tea and drinks. She would make gallons of gale beer, with bog myrtle gathered from the moors at Lowna and bottle it ready for the harvest months.

Gale beer was a volatile mixture, especially when freshly bottled and it was not unheard of for the corks to do real damage as they flew out of the bottles!

The corn was cut and the binder, drawn by four horses, made sheaves of corn, which then had to be hand-stooked to keep

Strickland and Billy Teasdale ploughing with horses.

it dry. These stooks were led into the yard later on and stacked ready for threshing.

These were very long days for everyone. Once the harvesting was done for the day, the family had to milk the cows in the evening; there was the stock to water and feed, as well as the care of the horses. They had to be fed, watered, brushed and settled down, at which point the family could finally eat dinner.

Rosie's neighbour, Tom, told of how they used to plough with two horses and aimed to cover one acre a day, which meant an average walk of 11 miles over the roughly ploughed surface, whilst also trying to stay within the furrow. Depending on what was being sown, the plough would usually have to go down 4 or 5 inches. The man also had to watch out for the handles of the plough. If the blades hit a rock, it would shake the wooden handles of the plough from side to side and, if the man standing between them wasn't quick to move, it would leave a bruise. So it was best to stand back, but that was harder work to hold them, as well as deal with two reins for the horses. Harrowing was even harder, designed to clear the land. The task of stone-picking was back-breaking work and meant covering a similar distance to the man with the horses. The children were expected to muck in together with the adults. During harvest 'you worked as long as you could see.'

Rosie's dad and other farmers would go up onto the moors, cutting turfs for the fire, working together. A 'boddin of cowls' were gathered for kindling from the moors at the same time. The cowls were the left-over stalks of heather, which had been burnt off. They were laid out in a row and tied up into a bundle with string to make the boddin, and they were carried home, slung over your shoulder. They

A Boddin o' Cowls

Whenivver Ah leeaks ower Rooaseberry way
Ah thinks of a cottage o'steean, dull and grey;
Mi grandad wi t'dog, cumin yam frev is wark,
An oppnin t'moor-yat just afoor it gat dark;
Mi granny at t'deear wiv a smahl - sha'd neea scowls -
Ti greet t'poor awd man wiv is boddin o' cowls.

Aye, monny a tahm when Ah gat yam fre skeeal -
Three mahl o' ard trampin it lay, doon i t'deeal -
Mi rabbits an pigeons an chicks fed for t'day,
Mi granny wad cum on ti t'deearstuns an say:
"It leeaks like a storm, arkstu noo oo it owls!
Gan meet thi awd grandad wi t'boddin o' cowls."

An noo of a moornin, aye, lang afoor six,
Ah oft es a scrat on ti finnd a few sticks;
Neea cowlins of gowlins or cowls, ling or whin,
Nay, neea bits o' nowt at 'll leet can Ah finn;
Neea wunder mi thowts to'ns ti yon poor awd sowls
At nivver was sho't of a boddin o'cowls!

An appen when Ah gits ower crammly ti wark,
An Ah've nowther foorman nor bosses ti nark,
They'll let me gan back ti t'lahl cot ower t'moor,
Wheer talliphone bells deean't ring oot oor bi oor.
If yah day ye pass an awd man at just crowls,
It cud easy bi me wiv a boddin o' cowls.

© Arthur Stanley Umpleby
A Cleveland Anthology, 1963 - Pg 18

50

burnt really well and were invaluable for log or turf fires. They also appeared in one of Rosie's favourite dialect poems.

Speaking of keeping the fire in, dead trees and branches were all cut up by hand with a cross cut saw. 'Dad always said logs warmed you twice; once when cutting and again when burning.'

In the spring, Rosie and her siblings would be given the job of planting taties. Her dad ploughed the field and then went back along the rows with a cart piling up heaps of manure. Rosie and her brothers would use a gripe to 'skell it about' and at the end of each row was a bag of seed potatoes. Gathering up a load into their course hessian aprons, they would drop a potato every foot up and down the field. Their dad would then follow along and infill with soil. The crop from these potatoes kept the family and pigs supplied for the year, with plenty left over to sell in Kirby.

Rosie thought pig killing day at the back end of the year was lovely. Not because she didn't like pigs, but because of what came out of the day's work. It was again a hard day, but every part of the animal was used, except its 'squeeak!' This kept the family going through the winter and meant they had ham for Christmas Day. In all, they killed three pigs to keep them through to spring.

After the pig was cut up, the family had supplies of black puddings, hams, bacon, sausages, lard for baking and cooking and Rosie's favourite – scrappings! These were chopped up pieces of skin, rendered down in the skillet, hung from the reckon and made crispy, a bit like pork scratchings today, but she loved to eat them with a bit of bread fresh from the pan. It was a meal in itself, not just a treat.

The pig's bladder was blown up and used to fill with lard and hang up in the eves at the top of the house to keep. If not used for that, it made a great football for the boys!

The hams were taken into the 'teefall' (pronounced teeafall) and laid out on the floor and covered with salt. Saltpetre was needed to keep the meat from going off. They were left for three weeks and then taken out to the dyke trough and washed. Once clean, a bit of band was tied round the shanks ends and left to drip for another two weeks. As soon as they stopped dripping, her dad hung them in the granary to keep them safe, although sometimes the mice did manage to get at them. If ever they needed a slice, then they went out with a carving knife and cut it off there and then.

The building regularly used to salt the pigs never really dried out; the salt seeped into the plaster and floors and even years later caused problems for those trying to get rid of it.

Thursday was bedroom day when the cleaning was done. The hooky rugs from the bedrooms were flung out of the windows and the wooden floorboards swept and then washed with carbolic soap. Only two rooms had the luxury of lino on the floor, and Rosie only made the mistake of polishing it once. After her dad slipped on the lino, no more was it to be polished. It took two of them to shake all the dust from the heavy hooky rugs, which then had to be rolled up and taken back up the stairs and put down for another week. And of course under the beds, the family kept apples, which Rosie and the others would 'scran' on a night-time.

Apart from the regular trimming of the oil lamps, the blackened ceilings had to be washed down. One hay-time Rosie remembered busily washing the beams down whilst up on the table. Her mam shouted "Quick Rosie, it's nearly lowance time! Mash the tea." But as Rosie filled the large teapot with the cast iron kettle, she spilt boiling water down her leg, scalding herself quite badly. Her mam put bicarbonate of soda onto the burns and that was it. No trip to the doctor's, as it all had to be paid for in those days - 10 shillings a time.

Stoneley Woods - Rudland - Kirbymoorside

Rosie remembered that Dr Galloway and Dr Jackson, who lived in Kirby, were the ones called out in emergency. Dr Jackson had his own chauffeur, Nathan Park, which was as well. Both men liked a drink, which was not uncommon in those days. There were never any official midwives either. The women helped each other out when the time came.

As a child, if you had a chesty cough, you could find yourself with a small bib smeared with goose grease and nutmeg, which had to stay on for weeks until the cough had gone. The family like many others relied on her mother's homemade remedies to treat all these kinds of ailments. But the goose grease stank to high heaven after a couple of weeks being rubbed on, back and front, every night.

Her dad would watch the sheep at the back end of the year and when they stood with their backs to the wind, it was a sure sign of bad weather on its way. He would take the family's horse and rulley down to Kirby station for some coal.

KIRBYMOORSIDE STATION.

Once at the station, his first task was to back the rulley onto the weighbridge (demolished in 2012) and a note taken of the weight. Then he manoeuvred the horse into the coal bay where the coal, which came straight from the mines, was loaded onto the rulley. This was then weighed again and her dad paid for the coal taken. All kinds of goods came into Kirby station and other produce such as fruit and livestock, including ducks, hens and turkeys, all from the Kirby area went out to the distant markets and towns.

Wednesday was market day and a busy day for all. People would gather to buy, sell and do deals. Horse and traps came from all round and they would be stabled in the King's Head and Black Swan. Rosie's dad would leave the horse and cart with the little old man there, who looked after them whilst he conducted the business of the day in the pub. One deal was 36-stone of wheat for a £1 from a corn agent. The man even got a whisky bought for him, which was a real result. Another deal was for two boxes of herring, 36 in all. However these had to be cleaned, washed and rolled once back home. It made a good meal with a bit of bread for the whole family. Her mam, alongside all the other farmers' wives, would sell eggs, butter and cheese for a bit of extra cash to buy things they couldn't grow or make themselves. Rabbits were a good source of income; she could get between 3 and 6 shillings for a pair at the market. And if her mam was ever short of meat come the weekend, she would say, "Get away and get a rabbit for dinner!" Rabbit stew with onion and carrots was a favourite and a staple part of the family diet - without the rabbit, many families would have really struggled to feed so many children.

As tenants of the Duncombe Estate, poaching of pheasants and deer from estate land and moors would have had dire consequences and may have even resulted in the family being evicted. The gamekeeper was Mr Fielder and as long as they only took from their own land, he wasn't bothered. So rabbits were a safe option.

Fox-hunting was important to the local farmers in those days. Rosie's neighbour, Tom Fletcher, knew all about the dangers of foxes. He always maintained they were difficult to shoot, as they are quick animals and had your scent before anyone had time to see them. Foxes would take lambs and poultry and one time Tom came home late to find that out of his 100 pullets, 40 were dead and only two actually taken. The fox would play with chickens before killing them. When they had cubs, the farmers had to be particularly careful with the poultry and again, once the youngsters had left the den. Tom even told of how a badger would take a lamb, when its teeth had worn down and it slowed with old age.

During the hunt, the fox would go to ground. On Boon Hill, the foxes had dug a hole into the yellow stone up on the top and it was extremely difficult to get them out of there. One time, the terrier put in to flush out the fox became stuck itself and the men spent all night trying to get it out. The fox left unharmed.

Winters were harsh. For Rosie and her family it was not unknown for them to be fastened in with the snow for up to eight weeks. One year snow came during Christmas week and Rosie didn't see the ground again until March. School would be shut down and the only people getting about were the men, who had to struggle through the snow on horseback or on foot.

Despite this, the stock had to be fed and watered. The sheep out in the fields were reliant on the hay gathered in the summer months and if this had been a good year, things were okay. During one particularly bad snowstorm, word came to the farm that one of Jackie Walkington's children was poorly and they were snowed in up at Allotments. With five children to feed, her mam sent Billie out with a basket of food and he set off. As Rosie watched from the window, the horse itself nearly got stuck as the snowdrifts were as high as the hedges.

At such times, there was nothing else to do but stay put. Once the stock was fed and watered, the family would gather in front of the roaring fire. Rosie remembered cutting up material to make the hooky rugs and quilts, sewing and knitting, as well as playing cards, draughts and dominos. The lamp glasses would be cleaned, ready for stabling up and the lads used to play Merrill's in the stables, where, amongst the warmth from the horses, they would carve out a board onto the top of a corn bin and amuse themselves for hours. They never came in for half the night.

In the summertime, the lads went to the Hope Inn at Rudland to play on the quoits pitch and would walk over to Hutton-le-Hole and Farndale to meet up with others to play. It was common to see up to 20 or more gathered for quoits at a time. Most villages had a cricket team and Rosie remembered the lads walking onto Nawton to watch or play in a match, but in Rudland quoits was the big passion.

The postman came every day, covering not only Rudland, but Sleightholmedale and Farndale; a letter posted on Monday would be back with a reply from London by Wednesday. The post came up from Kirby to Fadmoor Post Office, before being taken round the dales by bicycle. It was the vital link to the outside world.

Chapel was a big part of Rosie and her family's life. The children would go to Sunday School, led by Potter Waind and held at Rudland. Mr Waind was a big man with a large moustache. He was known to grab a knee if he saw they weren't paying attention, which hurt! The organ was played by Jack Waller, who pumped the bellows with his feet. The congregation would often hold camp meetings out in the open air and anniversaries called for Rosie to recite and memorise her piece for chapel. Tom Fletcher was another local man, who was their Sunday School teacher.

During the summer, the organ would be brought out of the chapel and set up in the wood and Rosie remembered vividly how nice it was hearing the singing through the trees, with the organ playing along. Of course in those days there weren't any cars going by or anyone to really notice them.

Rosie seated far right in 1921

The horses had to be taken along to Fred Dowson the blacksmith at Gillamoor to be shod, although her dad could do a few things himself. Rosie used to handle them and had her own pony and small donkey cart.

One day, as she was driving along the road, her dad called to her to fetch a bag of basic (pronounced 'bassic') slag back with her. This was a type of lime, made from the phosphorus-rich waste produced at the steelworks on Teesside.

However, the weather was dry and the ground hard, and just as he called out, the boards on the cart dropped, startling the pony which promptly bolted. It took off with Rosie struggling just to hold it. They rounded a corner, then over a small beck at which point she lost control. Her foot caught in the reins and she was dragged a short distance before the reins snapped. The pony, now in full flight, jumped a six spell gate, destroying the gate and cart. By the time everyone had got themselves and Rosie gathered up, the pony was trembling at the stable door, still attached to the shafts with only two wheels remaining. Fortunately, Rosie was only badly skinned and had to miss her recitation in chapel that night. She was determined however to get back on; the next day she saddled him up and rode out.

Cherry Tree Farm

A horse will always head for home if frightened, to wherever it feels safe.

Something similar happened to local man, Jack Green. He decided to yoke a henhouse to his horse - however the horse had never pulled anything like that before. It took fright at the shed attached by some chains and galloped across two fields, straight into its stable. Unfortunately, the henhouse stayed attached and jammed the horse up against the wall and Jack and the others had a terrible time trying to get in to take the chains off!

In times of trouble, family had to help each other. It was common for grandparents and other elderly relatives to be taken in by other family and all live together. Respect for your elders was drilled into the children and it was not accepted to call an older person by their Christian name.

On a Tuesday, Rosie would be sent over to help her sister Ellen, who lived at Skiplam Grange, when the housework at home was finished. She would ride over on her pony and come back at night.

Accidents on the farm were not uncommon. One of the Handley lads lost a foot in a threshing machine and William Willoughby lost an eye, working at Cherry Tree Farm in Sleightholme Dale, when he slid down the haystack and landed on an upturned hayfork. Circular saws were responsible for the loss of many a finger. Rosie's brother Jackie lost his thumb, but never let it stop him creating all kinds of treen items. He caught rheumatic fever when he was around 18 years old and had to be nursed at home by his mother. He spent the time carving a stack-prod, which was used to fasten the coverings over the haystacks, into a chain, using just a penknife.

One Rudland family Rosie remembered suffering more than most, were the Willoughby's, who lived at Hope Inn Farm. Hannah Wilson, from Rudland, married Harry Smith Willoughby, from Helmsley, in 1910 and moved in with her mother Hannah. They had their first daughter Kathleen shortly after, but she tragically died aged just 12 months. The couple had another six children, but lost their second son Percy at the age of four months in 1916, the same year as Hannah's mother died at the age of 76.

The family moved from Common Cottage to Hope Inn Farm, where they lived until 1924. William, the eldest son, was particularly clever and attended Gillamoor school where he sat his exams. Sadly, he came home one day to find his mother had committed suicide aged just 40.

Sykes House Rudland

With no other option, the children had to be taken in by the workhouse, and their father struggled on alone for another six months, before he too took his own life at the age of 38. The legacy of that tragedy was too much for some of their children, who struggled in adult life.

Thankfully, such family tragedies were few and far between. Rosie's mam cared for both her mother and father as they grew infirm. She remembered her grandfather, Strickland Walkington, was always singing little ditties as he kept the family in a ready supply of kindling. He had a long white beard and always put a lot of salt on his food. When told this, his reply was that if you didn't eat salt "you'd be eaten up with worms!"

Earlier in his working life, Strickland had led wood with a horse and cart and, along with Charlie Green and other local farmers, had broken stones for the council. They led stone from the local quarries at Sleighholme, Kirkdale, but only Bransdale and Rudland Rigg had blue flint stone. The

Teasdales and Greens were the last families to work the quarries at Rudland, ending with start of the First World War.

The quarried stone had to be taken by horse and cart and left in piles along the roadside for the men, who would sit on a small stool and hammer the stone to break it into usable sizes to fill the potholes. The farmers would be paid for this work, but not so for those from the workhouse, who gave their labour as repayment for their keep.

After the outbreak of war, life changed. Rosie remembered watching a German Zeppelin coming down the valley from Bilsdale and heading towards York, where it was brought down. However for the most part, families in the dales were relatively protected by their isolation and occupations.

Farmers were needed as much as soldiers.

After WWI, tramps, or roadsters, were regularly seen in and around the area. During the winter they sheltered in the workhouses, but as soon as the weather improved these characters took to the roads.

As well as Bill Kips, there was another local man from Kirby Mills who visited the dales. He would fill his bags and load his bicycle with all manner of goods to sell such as kippers, nuts, apples and oranges; anything he thought they would buy from him.

Rosie remembered one particular 'gadgie', known locally as Two Tups. His name was given to him, after he was heard shouting it out whilst crossing a field of sheep. He would wash in Hodge Beck and occasionally wash out his clothes there. Her dad would let him sleep in the cow shed, after removing his smokes from him. He always worried about fire. Her mam would fill his old can with tea and give him some food as he passed through. He came once a month and carried all he owned in a pack on his back. He looked a lot older than he would be, and always had a long straggly beard. Rosie presumed he had been a military man at some point as he always tried to keep himself tidy and acted reasonably to all he met.

Strangely enough, he could always find monkey nuts in his pack and would throw them to the children whenever he passed by the school or farms.

Some tramps had a code of honour. One tale tells of a wife who left some pies out on the windowsill to cool. A passing tramps pinched one, but as he met another traveller heading back towards the farm, he graciously asked if the man would return the dish to the windowsill, minus the pie.

ꞁ Valuation Day at Stonely Woods - how much for the midden?

Not all tramps received such a tolerant welcome. At the top end of Farndale, local legend has it that one such tramp wandered into a farmhouse where the wife was on her own and he refused to leave. She had been rendering lard on the fire and was so frightened by the intruder that she took matters into her own hands. When he fell asleep on the settee, she grabbed a funnel and poured some of the lard down his throat!

The outcome was not good and the story goes his body ended up buried in the midden heap, with no-one to know anything had gone on. Who would miss such a person, especially in those days and who is to know if it really happened or was simply told to deter potential intruders?

In 1935 Rosie married Percy Magson and moved from the farm into one of three cottages down Piercy End, at the bottom of the street near the Catholic church. These cottages have since been demolished, but were close to the foundry. As a result, black smuts would dirty her washing as they drifted over. Mr Rivis, a local joiner, made her a clothes horse as a wedding present, so she could dry the washing inside. Mr & Mrs Moss lived opposite, who also owned the laundry. Her husband, Percy, went to work for Thompsons, whose farmyard was opposite Stricklands.

Like much of rural Ryedale, Kirkbymoorside saw little direct action from the Germans. However, one day Percy was home for lunch and Rosie heard some buzzing about in the skies. She asked him not to go back to work, but Percy said not to worry because it was too foggy for them to try anything. A short while later, four bombs fell on the railway station and laundry. Thankfully two didn't go off, but the people in Duncombe Terrace and the bottom of Piercy End were moved out whilst the bombs were cleared.

Rosie could also remember the evacuees coming from Middlesbrough on the train into Kirby Station. They were marched up Piercy End and she was very moved at the sight of all these little children, hand in hand, with their gas masks round their necks, making their way up to the Memorial Hall.

She had decided not to go up because she wouldn't have been able to choose between them all. She already had her little daughter Shirley and the family only had two bedrooms, so there was no extra bedroom. However, at the end of the day, the vicar knocked on her door and she found herself being asked to take in a little boy - he was the only one left and if no-one would take him, he would be sent home.

Rosie was too kind-hearted to say no and agreed to take him in. That boy was called John Hardy and he lived with them for two years; he proved himself to be a lovely lad and caused them no trouble at all. He visited a few times after the war and last she heard, he was joining the navy.

Percy didn't go into the Army as he was in a reserved occupation, but he did join the Civil Defence and received a medal in recognition for his efforts during the war. After their second daughter, Kathleen, was born, the family moved up to the newly-built Swedish timber houses in Ryedale View, where she took in a lodger, Mr Bright, a local policeman.

To earn a little extra, Rosie worked at the Adela Shaw Hospital on nights, and took in washing, charging 6d a shirt. When the hospital closed in 1970, she worked nights at the Old Folk's Home, Dale End House. She became an ardent supporter of the Royal British Legion, and spent 40 years raising funds through the poppy appeals and in 2009 was given a trip to the Royal Albert Hall.

In 2003, Rosie received the Eminent Citizen's Award from the Kirkbymoorside Town Council and she also spent a lot of effort raising money for Cancer Research and The Soldiers' and Sailors' Children's Appeal.

The Ryedale Folk Museum often turned to her to work with children and adults on a variety of projects relating to the local dialect and history of the area. Her brother Jackie was involved at the very beginning of the museum, along with Bert Frank. To commemorate this support, the Ryedale Folk Museum named a study room after her, another proud moment in her life.

Rosie died in 2014 at the age of 100 - her philosophy on life:

"I can't grumble about my life - it's been hard work, but it's keeping going, that keeps you going."

Fireside Tales

This is a transcript of Harry Rickaby chatting to Ivy Sturdy about their childhood memories.

I remember the dances held in the Church House, there would be 12 dances, an interval, and then another 12 – the evening would end around one or two in the morning. The MC would wear white gloves and couples had to dance the correct way round the hall. The local clubs, the golf, tennis and cricket club all held dances and I remember once going to the Golf Club Ball when they had Terry's of York doing the catering. I remember it cost 10/6d. If anyone wanted the bands to play on after time, the hat would go round the room to pay for it!

And I can remember at one time there were five billiard tables in Kirkby; there was Church House, the Literary Institute and the Dug-out where the Old Comrades used to gather, it was set up after the First World War.

Ryedale Show always used to have a different venue each year, they would rotate between Pickering, Helmsley and Kirkby. When it came here, it would be held on West Fields, near to where they built the new school.

Didn't they use to have some good bands come for the occasion? The Black Dyke Mills and such like would march from the Market Place to the show field. Dances were held in the evening, and there would be other things on, such as running races and dog races.

Of course we also had the cinema in those days. My dad used to set up the films on our kitchen table. We would show the Pathé news, two reels of comedies followed by an hour and a half film. I used to play the piano to accompany them and I had my own repertoire of music for certain ones. My dad fixed up a battery to run the projector. To start with there were only wooden benches for people to sit on, with handles at each end so we could move them. Of course the children sat on forms at the front. In the beginning we had to change the reels, but later on it changed so there were no breaks in the films.

What can you remember playing as a child?

We were forever outside, climbing trees in Manor Vale; I would play dolls and we made dens in the Mary Render on the hills. Of course on school days I had to wash the teapots first, before being allowed out. Mum always said to listen out for the church clock and be home by 8pm. We played hopscotch outside on the street and sometimes boules, the boys had iron hoops and loved to spin tops on the pig pens.

And of course in those days everyone walked for pleasure as well as work; whole families went out on a Sunday for a walk.

Do you remember, we used to be able to go straight over the hills? There was a footpath that took you to Rumsgill, Jubilee Walk it was called; but Holts changed all that.

Ivy Blackburn, 1908

Were there any other place names you can remember?

There were the banks....First Bank was where we would pick strawberries and gather up ash sticks for the fire. The second was called Rumsgill Bank and then the third was called Leg of Mutton; after that you came out at Gillamoor Lime Kiln, where we spent hours playing.

There was a seat by the pond on Viver's Hill near the Mary Render, wasn't there?

Yes; and Jacky Jackson had cows up there and used to bring them through the streets. But you see Jackson's farm was behind Church House. Connings had cows as well, but they were kept over the other side of the bridge.

And Thompson's Farm is now called Ginger Hall and they brought their cows through the streets as well. There was always plenty of cow muck about for manure.

Can you remember the pubs in Kirkby? We had the George & Dragon, Black Swan, King's Head and the White Swan.

That was for the men, in my day there were no women in the pubs, not really...

We went to the Women's Institute, there were the sewing and knitting clubs. Kirkby had a drama group and the Franks would hold musicals and concert parties. People used to come from far away to perform and listen.

And I remember Miss Wood had a knitting machine and she would knit socks.

Freddie Clark used to play the piano - Spoony as he was called. His granddad had an open carriage and the boys would love to hang off the back. Whenever someone shouted at him, Mr Clark would flick his whip and the boy wouldn't half feel it if the whip caught him.

Jim Clark was also the drayman and he had two sisters if I remember right. What I can remember is that there was always a fight whenever the Kirkby lads played football against Helmsley.

We had some characters back then. Walter Tateson from Crown Square – he was a horseman and had ponies on the beach at Sandsend and Redcar. He broke horses in as well.

Then of course there was Mrs Baker in Crown Square – Harriet – didn't she originally marry Jacob Winter? Queen of the Gypsies they used to call her.

Oh, Tommy Baker was a hard man and a fighter too. He knocked everyone out. I once had a fight with him round the back of Hodgson's Garage; of course that's where all the fights took place. I was lucky and caught him off guard and knocked him down.

I remember going to a dance up at Guisborough Grammar School one time and in the pub afterwards, someone came up to me and asked if I was the Harry who had flattened Tommy Baker. It made me a bit of a hero, it seems, but it really was only a lucky punch that did it. Tommy came from Guisborough. Do you remember the hirings in Kirkby?

Oh yes. There was the Martinmas Fair when they would come with the roundabouts, hoop-la, coconut shies and they had wrestling as well. That was the Winters from Guisborough way. The men would try their strength on the hammer, and of course the Cake Walk, that was something! But in those days the fair filled the Market Place and went all the way up to the Church House. Although I was only little, I clearly remember hearing the animals, which came in cages – the lions used to roar and it's a sound I can still hear now.

Do you remember the men looking for work then, at the fairs?

The men would come down from Farndale and Bransdale for the hirings. Of course Martinmas was change-over day. They would be home for a couple of weeks and then back to work for the year. It was also hair-cut time!

I don't remember women at the hirings

They would be there but they worked in the house. Women would bake twice a week in those days and made their own cheese.

What else can you remember Ivy?

When we moved into the house in the main market place, every bonfire night we would have a bonfire on the cobbles outside our house. Lots of the folk would come and join us and we let off fireworks. Our Lynn never liked all the bangs so I always had to take her back in.

What about the shops back then?

We had plenty of things in town. There was a cake shop in Dale End run by Sugar Annie as she was known. Her real name was Annie Hodgson and she also sold sweets. Not that she was very sweet, she was tight and I remember always wore a shawl. Us kids called her nip currant.

Ivy Sturdy with baby Judy

And once a week Will Hutchinson went and collected a box of kippers off the train and sold them. He would shout of "Kip" as he came along. He worked as a gardener as well, lived up Gillamoor Road.

Mrs Charter sold pots and there was Ellerkers in West End – they were gardeners and had a greengrocer's there.

Harry Rickaby at Ivy's 90th birthday bash

Another thing, do you remember the fire engine, which was kept in Crown Square? It was near the church steps, but the horse to pull it was kept up Swineherd Lane.

What about school Ivy?

I never cared much for school, but I did enjoy needlework and cookery.

I remember Mr Donkin was headmaster back when I went to Kirkby school. He wasn't much liked, another hard man. He broke the skin on my hand one time when I got the cane. When my father saw it, he went in and had a strong word with him. He went onto a school in Skinnigrove.

We used to get up to some mischief. I remember me and my mates liked to play tricks on Ned Humble. We would tie a button onto a piece of cotton or string and used it to knock on his windows. Eventually he worked it out and waited upstairs for us. When we got close enough, he emptied the chamber pot out the window onto us!

Another time I shot a bird off the top of a chimney pot with my catapult. I was really pleased with myself until the police called round home later that evening to tell me off. It seems the bird fell down the chimney and landed in someone's pan which was on the fire!

You know the Suddaby's from Malton? One time Fred Potter, the policeman, arrested Bobby Suddaby for fighting and took him to the cells in Tinley Garth. One of the lads who went with him, pinched the Inspector's walking stick. The inspector always carried a walking stick.

You know what – that lad was my brother-in-law Vivian! He kept that walking stick for years!

There was one Sergeant in town and two constables. They used to do point duty in the Market Place. Sergeant Chisholme always stood in the middle, where the streetlight is now. That's why they call it Chisholme's monument. My dad used to say he was "like a streak of pump water."